QuiCleanse

AUTHOR NAME:

Joey Gallardo Jr.

&

Andy Gallardo

ISBN:069260555X
ISBN-13:9780692605554

DEDICATION

We want to dedicate this book to our parent's, whom without them we could not have start this journey. Our parent's gave us the opportunity to open three locations with a little blood, sweat, and tears. We have managed to successfully make healthy lifestyles for others and change people's lives for the past nine years. Thank you mom and dad Gallardo.

Any support system will work, if you believe you can do it!!

CONTENTS

1. _QUICLEANSE BENEFITS_

This is an opportunity… This is an opportunity for you to make a serious health change. If you are ready to make some changes to yourself that will improve your quality of life you have come to the right place! I have been in the fitness industry for more than 15 years and I have a passion for helping people so I developed Quicleanse. Quicleanse helps empower you by giving you the proper tools you need to make yourself a new lifestyle, incorporating health and fitness. Always, contact a health care professional before beginning any new health program to ensure that it is appropriate for your health needs.

This program has taken my organization many years to show continuous success with my clients, friends, and family. Quicleanse can show you how to lose 5 to 10 pounds of body fat, the quick and easy way, in one week. Quicleanse detox program will eliminate body fat and assist to maintain your weight loss through. The Quicleanse organization can help eliminate Visceral

Body Fat in just one week. We want to share this gift of health and fitness with all who seek the source of the inner happiness and personal peace. Quicleanse helps empower you by giving you the proper tools needed for achieving a new lifestyle in health and fitness. This organization will help educate, motivate, and help you meet your realistic goals using a scientific approach to bring out the inner you.

Our elite program is able to meet your own customized health and fitness goal.

What does Quicleanse Program actually do for me?

Do you want better, overall health? In today's world it is nearly impossible to stay away from all harmful toxins and chemicals. They exist in the air we breathe, the food, and water that we all consume. There are potential toxins and chemicals in a large amount of our basic everyday nutritional intake. These toxins build up in our system faster than our organs can carry them out. When this "build up" process begins we start feeling symptoms.

Symptoms can present in many different ways and severity but here are some of the ways your body is telling you there is a "build

up:" Allergies, Depression, Weight Problems, Arthritis, Asthma Fatigue, Ingestion, Anxiousness, Bad Breath, Lack of focus, Hypertension, Sinus problems, and these are just a few of the more common issues that can present from a buildup of toxins.

By using this Quicleanse program you will start to feel more positive and your energy will increase. These changes are the first signs your body is healing and your organs are starting to function better. The removal of toxins and waste from your system will also help with more restful sleeps, faster metabolism, decreased severity in diabetes, positive thoughts, stronger immune system, and you can lose 5 to 15 pounds of Visceral body fat. Quicleanse is holistic detox program to help eliminate visceral body fat in one week. This program will help kick start you to a healthy lifestyle. You become successful the minute your start moving towards a worthy goal. IT all begins with the first step and the first plan. Planning for the future can be difficult but start some future plan now. Quicleanse will help you develop some basic plans for your detox program, adapt them as needed, and always consult with you

Primary Care Doctor or other medical professional before beginning any new program to ensure positive outcomes.

The best day of my life

(This quote best signifies the Quicleanse motivation and why Quicleanse is the company it is)

"This is the beginning of new day. I have seen given this day to use as I will. I can waste it or use it for good. What I do today is important because I am exchanging a day of my life for it. When tomorrow comes, this day will be gone forever, leaving in its place whatever I have traded for it.

I pledge to myself that it shall be:

Gain, not loss

Good, not evil

Success, not failure in order that I shall not regret the price I paid for this day."

2. *Your Mind Cleanse*

Let's go over the mind changing process. You have already begun to change the way you think about health and nutrition if you are exploring this book and hopefully others. It can be intimidating and overwhelming to see all of the different option available to the public regarding health and nutrition. You have already begun the process of changing YOU just by considering new information. That is wonderful and congratulations! Think about who you are and who you want to be can be a very humbling time and it is easy to get lost in the negative emotions of it all. Changing your ways to eliminate visceral body fat is just one part to your weight loss journey. Whatever the reason you want to lose weight it starts with you!

You first start to explore the health benefit or health conditions to weight loss. This is why you're here with Quicleanse organization to lose 5 to 10 pounds of visceral body fat. I will always tell clients my theory of "Cause and Effect." In order to make a changes in your life, you must identify your reason to change. Is the emotional connection positive or negative? What we mean by the emotional connection is do you feel like you have to lose or that you want to be healthier, the mindset of a person is the best indicator of positive results.

The plan is to ask and answer these following questions: What is driving me lose weight? Do I have the support to make the changes that I want? Is your family on board because the meal changes will impact everyone? Do you have someone or something that can help you stay motivated? Some people get held up in this **Pre-contemplation** stage. Pre-contemplation where the person needs feedback of their own views to a state an awareness.

Contemplation stage is where we tend to reflect positive statements to help everyone reach the decision, whatever that decision may be, about changes in their detox phases. Positive energy and feeling good about the change is key. There will be times when you want to stop/quit that's where the motivation behind the change and support system come in. The next two stages of the change cycle are **Preparation and Action.** These two stages are where people tend to experiment with all the ideas in their head. It can be easy to get lost here because there are so many options. A key to eliminating some of the options is to understand where you are in your life right now. There are distractions everywhere so be aware of your reality and not the "perfect" mindset that you may be holding on to. This means making a plan for your level of needs, your abilities, your motivation, and support system. Act on the simple plan to meet the first goal. The first step will lead to another positive step and so on. When thinking about making your goals, the first step could just be to drink more water every day to work up to drinking the 8 glasses a day. Most people don't realize how dehydration contributes to their aches, pains, and illnesses.

Here are a couple questions that may be running through your mind right now: How can I accomplish the first goal? How am I going to keep meeting my goals in the days, months, and years to come? The first step is realizing that as long as you try you cannot fail. Once we are able to take the possibility of failure out of the equation it is easier to move forward and meet the daily goals. When a plan is set to be in motion then it is now possible to move forward and begin making a bigger change. When you get to the maintenance process things get a little tricky. The maintenance process is where you have reached some of your goals and are maintaining your objective. It can be difficult to stay on task with all of the goals but later we will discuss some helpful tips to getting through it and making permanent changes to better your health.

Those who say "it cannot be done should not interrupt the people doing it!" A positive support is the key to most success stories, in any area of life. If you don't have a support system, then make it a goal to develop one. Humans tend to be "pack people" and will tend to gravitate to people that think like them. Make it a goal to expand your horizons and learn about differences; people, places, or anything. Learning different exercises and breathing techniques can be very helpful when embarking on a new health program.

Remember, feed your mind and body good things to promote

growth. WHERE DO YOU SEE YOURSELF ON CHART?

THE STAGES OF CHANGE

Precontemplation	Contemplation	Determination/ Preparation	Action	Maintenance	Relapse/ Recycle
NO	?	YES	GO!	CRUISING	UGH

Where do you see yourself in the process of change?

3. *POSITIVE CHANGES*

Throughout this process you will go through various stages of positive change both mentally and physically. In completing this process, you will not only better your physical health but your mental health as well. You will feel more energy and may sleep better at night. Yes, there will be inches lost and happier days on the scale. You may even notice that your hair and nails are healthier, less brittle. You will see your energy increase more and more over time and you should notice a change in taste buds as well. You will find that you no longer crave those unhealthy foods that may have been a large part of your eating habits previously. This change can be as big or as bigger as you want it to be... Less eating out means more family time at home around the table. More energy can mean you increase your workout or add something new or just increases the ability to keep up with your kids or friends. Cleansing yourself of toxins and being healthier will lead to mood changes and overall mental clarity. You will find

that you are able to remember more and may not feel as stressed.

You will be able to focus and may experience changes to your

mood. Often times when they are leaving the body an individual

will feel generally happier. The happy endorphins will be flowing

and things that may have bothered you before no longer have the

same effect. There is growing evidence that suggests a healthy

diet of natural foods will reduce anger, depression, anxiety, and

certain sleep disorders. Stay Positive and Happy! Remind

yourself, you are worth it!.

4. _TOXINS AND EFFECTS_

What stops us from being able to achieve the weight loss goal?
Every person's body responds differently to the type and amount
of stimulation that you are applying towards your weight loss
program. The bottom line is that you need to find out what is the
right combination to unlock your fat burning potential. The most
important key is to know the right amount of time you need to
recover. For example, more time in the gym is not necessarily the
best answer to lose weight, sometimes less is more. Researchers
have found short bursts of exercise with a short rest period permits
the body to burn more fat and build lean muscle.

During the detox process you may find yourself irritable, going to
the bathroom a lot more, and achy. You will want to stop and get
back to feeling comfortable but remind yourself that comfortable is
where you were and it wasn't where you wanted to be. I will more
of toxins and there effects it in Chapter 5. Stay Positive and
Happy! Remind yourself, you are worth it!.

5. *THE 7-DAY QUICLEANSE*

You first have to adjust your mental awareness for this journey into a new lifestyle of health. It will be an injustice to clean your temple (body) if you do not have a support system set up to maintain your eating, exercise, and sleeping cycles. You can make small adjustments toward you're eating habits that will feel, taste, and do better in your digestive system.

What will a natural Detox program do for my overall health?

This is where you will get rid of the "build up" that we touched on earlier. Remember your body is talking to you and telling you what is wrong with it. Listen to your body and make sure to complete your regular physicals and check-up with your primary care physician or nurse practitioner. Staying on top of your health and knowing what to look for will help you achieve your goals. With all the preservatives and chemicals in our food, water, and air it is almost impossible to not ingest some type of chemical or toxin.

When our body becomes out of balance with the chemicals and toxins we start to show symptoms of this toxicity. Here are some examples:

ALLERGIES DEPRESSION WEIGHT PROBLEM

ARTHRITUS LUPUS ASTHMA FATIGUE

INDIGESTION AXIETY BAD BREATH

LACK OF FOCUS HYPERTENSION SINUS PROBLEM

HEADACHES HORMONE IMBALANCE

The first positive change you will feel from your body detox program will be an increase of energy because your organs will function better. The removal of this toxic waste from the system will help with:

DIABETES FASTER METABOLISM

RESTFUL SLEEP

POSITIVE THOUGHTS

= STRONGER IMMUNE SYSTEM

LESS UNHEALTHY FOOD CRAVINGS

AND YOU WILL LOSE 5 TO 15 POUNDS OF

VICERAL BODY FAT.

Here is an example of a nutritional plan to detox your body

You can eliminate 5-15 pounds of body fat off your system in one week with our entire detox program. Supplements are required to sustain your vitamin, mineral, and antioxidant levels. Talk to your doctor to determine which supplement works best for you. The supplement must be accompanied by a cardio routine and time in an Infrared Sauna for the duration of 5 days in a row. Always, contact a health care professional before beginning any new health program to ensure that it is appropriate for your health needs. Specifically ask your doctor about the possible health effects for you regarding the Infrared Sauna as heat can be harmful with certain medical issues and medications.

Ask your doctor before beginning any new health program, make sure to inform your doctor about any preexisting conditions.

The Quicleanse Plan: for 7 Days

Wake Up: Lemon Juice with 6-8 oz. of water.

6-9am   Breakfast: Protein shake: 2 oz. Rice/Soy milk, ½ cup fruit, 1 tablespoon of raw oats and flax meal, a dash of cinnamon, 6-8 oz. water.

10-12am   **Snack**:   4-8 sticks of celery with black beans or hummus.

12-2pm   Lunch: A veggie soup, with a side of ½ cup brown rice with broccoli and a small amount of yogurt or apple sauce.

3-5pm   Snack: 4-8 sticks carrots with black beans or hummus.

6-9pm   Dinner: Lentils with Quinoa; or mixed green salad with red bell peppers.

Before Bed: Protein shake, no fruit, milk, or oats. 6-8 oz. water, cinnamon, and flax meal.

Some of the AM ingredients .

Some of the PM ingredients.

6. *BODY CLEANSE SAMPLE*

This chapter takes us through the body work-outs and quick exercise programs to help get started and maintain throughout your transition. These exercises will help condition and strengthen your body.

There are many workout routines available from various sources and all can work for some individuals and not for other. It can get very confusing at times.

In case you are unfamiliar with fitness terminology here are a couple terms to know and understand. When you complete all the exercises one time that is one "set." Reps, or repetitions, are the number of times one motions is completed. 10 crunches you have done 10 repetitions/ reps. If you do this 3 times you have completed 3 sets of 10 reps. For instance, if your goal is to tone and shape your body use light weights and complete more reps.

Here is an example of a basic routine that can be changed as needed and is relatively easy to implement in your everyday life:

3 sets of 10 Repetitions can be done with any type of exercise, with or without weight. Before beginning any sets make sure to warm up with 15 minutes of cardio. Cardio is any movement that gets your heart rate up to improve oxygen intake by the body. Cardio not only helps you lose or maintain weight, it helps you build stamina so you can remain active for a longer period of time.

If and when you find yourself ready to incorporate weight and really start to trim and fine tune your body this exercise routine will get you on your way:

Complete 4 sets. 1st set is 12 reps with two standard cans from the pantry, 5 pound weight, or a 5 pound exercise band. 2nd set is 10 reps with 1 10 pound bag of potatoes, 10 pound weight, or a ten pound exercise band. 3rd set is 8 reps with 15 pounds. The weight used is whatever you can do. The goal is to stress your body in a healthy way, just make sure to increase the weight each set.

Basic Work -Out Options

1. Jumping Rope
2. Jumping Jacks

3. Wall Sit (with or without weight)

4. Push – UP

5. Abdominals Crunch (with or without weight)

6. Leg Lunge (with or without weight)

7. Traditional Plank

8. High Knees/ Running in place (with or without weight)

9. Side Planks

10. Triceps dip on using a single chair

11. Air Punches (with or without weight)

To end the workout STRETCH! It is important to stretch after every workout to reduce soreness and improves circulation. Make sure to stretch the muscles that you used particularly well in addition to stretching all the rest of your body. Stretching allows your body to begin the cool down process. If you cool down too quickly it can lead to muscle strain, cramping, and feeling like you have the flu.

Drinking water is vital to your success. You have to keep your body hydrated. If there's nothing keeping your body lubricated it will break and grind to a halt. If you are supposed to drink 8 glasses of water on an average day, with the workouts provide above, it is now necessary to drink at least 12 glasses of water every day. There are many ways to remind yourself and measure how much water you are taking in. If you want some suggestions please go to our website: www.quiccleanse.org

Ask your doctor before beginning any new health program, make sure to inform your doctor about any preexisting conditions.

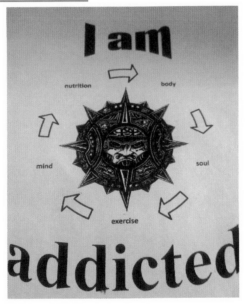

7. *WHAT TO DO AFTER*

Do you ever wonder why some diets do not work for people who want to lose weight? One of the main reasons is due to our foods that contain toxins, growth hormones, additives, preservatives, and high levels of sugars which are put into our bodies currently. If you are not careful your body will then store these dangerous items as visceral body fat. This body fat will attach itself to vital organs, which can cause them to not function properly. This can hold back your metabolism from burning off the proper calories your body needs to sustain itself and to help lose the unwanted weight. In order to burn off the extra weight you must consider several factors such as: age, sex, lifestyle, genetic disorders, and injuries.

How can I accomplish my goal **NOW?** Future planning is a key element to success. Begin making future plans for your new routine and how to continue the exercise and nutritional program beyond the short term goals? Once you have this plan in place it is time to manifest your short term goals.

The maintenance process is where you have reached some of your goals and are maintaining your objective. If your first goal is to drink more water to get to 8 glasses of water every day and you meet that goal, you continue to drink 8 glasses of water every day this is called maintenance or maintaining the change. You should have gone though some mental, spiritual, and physical changes throughout the process it took to get you feeling better about your new methods. This stages are the hardest to stay focused. Here are some tips to use during your cleansing cycle to help stay on track:

How can I control my Appetite so I can lose more weight?

The biggest reason we tell people to document their food intake is so they can see how their metabolism is responding to their eating habits. There are certain factors to consider that may be the root of the problem; lack of sleep, DNA, Stress, Bio-Chemistry (Leptin, Insulin, Ghrelin, Melatonin), even Micro-bacteria in our digestive systems. Here are some helpful hints to gain control over those bad eating habits:

Why do I keep losing weight only to gain it right back?

A common problem among the general public is the idea of weight loss programs being miracle cures and guarantees. Most simply believe that a diet, a fabulous supplement, and an exercise routine will cancel out all of the bad eating behaviors. When a person is unable to overcome bad eating habits which are driven by internal dilemmas they will be more likely to gain the weight back. Issues that generally cause people to slip back a few steps:

1. Food Addiction

2. Use of food as a mothering comfort substitute

3. Emotional Eating

4. Loss and Deprivation of Spiritual needs

5. Inadequate stress management skills

6. Unresolved childhood trauma

With proper instruction, motivation, and self-management they can be conquered as long as you have a well-informed plan to follow.

Some concerns may need to be addressed by a professional for permanent resolution.

Most so called "trainers" or weight loss experts cannot identify or relate to their clients' needs. The trainer feels that the client needs to step up their level of fitness. I have found and believe in my own theory, "YOU must have a CAUSE in order to have an EFFECT." In 15 years of experience, we have proven a 90% success rate with clients. In the first week with our Quicleanse Body Detox program, we will help you lose 5-15 pounds of body fat, not including

- Go through a proper body cleanse program.

- Start a food and exercise journal

- Eat about three meals and three snacks (veggies, fruits, nuts) per day.

- Potion your plate with about 15g-20g of protein per meal.

- Chew gum instead of eating sweets.

- Drink about 1 liter of Green Tea throughout the day...

- Get 6-8 hours of deep sleep.

- Exercise for about 30-45minutes a day.

- Start a daily food and exercise journal.

- Get your family involved by eating healthier diet.

- Find a workout buddy to help kick start change. (There is a comfort in numbers)

- Keep setting up deadlines for your short term goals.

- Schedule a daily workout into your daily routine.

- Find solutions to your excuses.

- Be Happy about what you have done so far.

- Stay POSTIVE and let go of the negative energy.

water weight.

<u>Ask your doctor before beginning any new health program, make sure to inform your doctor about any preexisting conditions.</u>

8. *QUICLEANSE MEAL RECIPE*

Here are some recipes to help you on your way. These are quick and easy to fix, making it easy to put these into your everyday routine. These recipes are healthy alternatives and the nutritional information for all recipes are at the end of each recipes. For more information and more recipes go to our website: www.quiccleanse.org.

Ask your doctor before beginning any new health program, make sure to inform your doctor about any preexisting conditions.

Breakfast

Apple French Toast
Serves 2

Ingredients
1 Apple Sliced
1 Egg Beaten
2 Slices Whole Wheat Bread
½ cup Apple Juice
1 tsp corn starch
Vanilla
Cinnamon
1 tbsp. Cold Water

Cook in a sauce pan the apple slices in the apple juice for 8 minutes or until tender.

Combine the egg and a splash of vanilla in a small bowl and mix well. Dip the bread in the egg until all of the egg is absorbed.

Cook the bread on both sides in a non-stick skillet. Remove the apple slices from the apple juice using a slotted spoon. Carefully arrange the apple slices on the toast.

Combine the corn starch and a dash of cinnamon and sugar, gradually blend with 1 tbsp. of cold water. Stir this combination in with the apple juice and heat on medium until the sauce begins to thicken. Spoon sauce over apples and serve.

Nutritional information for 2 slices
180 Calories
16g Carbs
3g Protein
4g Fat
2g Sugars

Poached Egg and Cheese Muffins

Serves 2

Ingredients
1 tsp Vinegar
2 Eggs
2 Slices of American Cheese
2 English Muffins

In a 1-quart pot fill ¾ full of water, add 1 tsp of vinegar, bring to a slow boil.

Place the English Muffins in the toaster. Break eggs and drop into the water, cook until egg whites are done. Turn off the heat and carefully scoop the eggs out of the pot. Place the eggs on the toasted English Muffins and cover with American cheese. Place the muffin crown on top and Serve.

Nutritional information for 1 Muffin
250 Carbs
24g Calories
13g Protein
9g Fat
2g Sugars

Steak, Eggs, and Potato

Serves 2

Ingredients
2 Potatoes
1 tsp. oil
2 Thin Cut Breakfast Steaks
¾ Cup Egg Beaters
2 tbsp. Worcestershire Sauce
Salt and Pepper

Peel and dice potatoes. Ina medium skillet heat 1 tsp. oil on medium heat and drop potatoes in. Stir occasionally until potatoes are desired coloring or a light brown. Reduce heat and cover, continuing to stir occasionally.

In a small bowl dab steaks in 2 tbsp. Worcestershire Sauce, seasoning with salt and pepper.

In a medium sized pan cook steaks thoroughly. In a small egg pan pour ¾ cup egg beaters. Stir while cooking until done.

Divide equally on 2 plates and serve.

Nutritional information for 2 Servings
270 Calories
5g Carbs
20g Protein
9g Fat
1g Sugars

Ham and Egg Burritos

Serves 2

<u>Ingredients</u>
2 low carb tortillas
3 eggs or ¾ cup egg beaters
2 slices ham
Onion and bell pepper (optional)

Dice ham and any vegetables desired and place in a small bowl.
Shell eggs and beat until well blended.

If using onion; heat ½ tsp oil in a small egg pan and sauté onion
until partially translucent. Toss in the ham and pour in the eggs.
Cook until eggs are desired tenderness, stirring occasionally.

Heat tortillas carefully either on a tortilla pan or in the microwave.

Spoon egg mixture on to tortillas evenly, add any desired
vegetables, and serve.

Nutritional information for 1 Burrito
With Eggs	With Egg Beaters
195 Calories	135 Calories
8g Carbs	3.5g Carbs
13g Protein	13g Protein
8g Fat	4g Fat
1g Sugar	1g Sugar

<u>Vegetable Scramble</u>

<u>Serves 2</u>

<u>Ingredients</u>
3 eggs or ¾ egg beaters
Green pepper
Onion
Any other desired vegetables
½ tsb oil

Dice desired vegetables. In a small bowl shell and beat eggs until well blended.

In a medium egg pan heat ½ tsb oil. Toss in vegetables. Heat, stirring occasionally, until the onions are translucent. Pour in eggs, cook on medium heat, until eggs are cooked to desired firmness.

Serve and ENJOY!

Nutritional information for 1 Serving
Egg   Egg Beater
130 Calories   65 Calories
5g Carbs   5g Carbs
10g Protein   10g Protein
7g Fat   2g Fat
2g Sugars   2g Sugars

Chef Salad
Serves 2

Ingredients
Romaine lettuce
Carrot
Tomatoes
Slices Ham
Sliced Turkey
2 Hard-boiled Eggs
Fat Free Dressing (any kind)

In a 1-quart pan, gently place two eggs in the pot and fill with water. Bring eggs and water to a fast boil. Boil eggs for 8-10 minutes, then drain, and allow to cool.
Wash 8 leaves of lettuce and cut into 1 inch squares.
Peel 1 carrot, cut in half, and shred ½ of the carrot.
Core and slice the tomato into 8 wedges.
Cut 4 slices of ham and 4 slices of turkey into small squares.
In a medium size bowl toss the lettuce and shredded carrot together.

Divide the mixture evenly onto 2 plates. Evenly divide the ham and turkey on top of the lettuce. Place the tomato wedges around the lettuce. Peel the cooled eggs, slice in half, and place the halves onto the plates. Top with your favorite Fat Free Dressing and ENJOY!

Nutritional information for 1 Serving
220 Calories
6g Carbs
22g Protein
7.5g Fat
2g Sugar

Club Sandwiches
Serves 2

Ingredients
Whole Wheat Bread
Sliced Turkey
Sliced Ham
Tomato
Lettuce
Fat Free Mayonnaise and/or Mustard
American cheese

Wash and slice 4 slices of tomato. Wash and peel 2 large leaves of lettuce.

Lay out 4 slices of bread, spread mustard, mayonnaise, or any combination onto the bread.

Layer ham, turkey, and 1 slice of cheese. Top with lettuce and tomato.

Slice and serve.

Nutritional information for 1 Sandwich
250 Calories
16g Carbs
18g Protein
8g Fat
6g Sugar

Beef/ Chicken
Stir Fry and Steamed Rice

Serves 2

Ingredients
2 Chicken Breast cut into strips
OR
10oz Beef Stir Fry

1 Red Bell Pepper
1 Green Bell Pepper
¼ Onion
Snow Peas
Instant White Rice
Water Chestnuts (optional)
1 ½ tbs. Teriyaki glaze (optional)

Slice the onions and bell pepper thin, about ½ inch wide be 1 ½ inches long.
Cut meat into pieces about 1-1 ½ inches long.
Start the Instant Rice following the instructions given on the box.
Heat the 1 tsp. oil in a large saucepan. Toss in the vegetables, stir well in oil then toss in the meat. Cook well until meat is done and vegetables are tender.
Spoon Stir Fry over white rice and serve.

If using Teriyaki glaze: When the meat is done, pour in 1 ½ tbs. Teriyaki glaze, and stir in well. Spoon over rice and serve.

Nutritional information

Chicken	**Beef**
389 Calories per serving	429 Calories per serving
42g Protein	25g Protein
41g Carbs	41g Carbs
7g Fat	15g Fat
3g Sugar	3g Sugar

Fajita Pita

Serves 2

<u>Ingredients</u>
1 Chicken Breast Fillet
  OR
8oz Beef Steak
2 Pita Halves
1 Onion
1 Tomato
1 Green Pepper
1 Lemon if using Chicken
1 Lime if using Beef
Salt and Pepper

Marinate chicken in lemon juice or, if using, beef marinate in lime juice. Cut onion, tomato, and green pepper into small strips. Season meat with salt and pepper and cook thoroughly. While the meat is cooking heat ¼ tsp oil in a small egg pan and toss in the vegetables. Sautee the vegetables until the onions are translucent. When the meat is completely cooked carefully cut into small strips. Divide the meat and vegetables equally into the pita pockets. Serve and enjoy!

Nutritional information for 1 Pita

Beef	**Chicken**
200 Calories	200 Calories
13g Carbs	13g Carbs
15g Protein	20g Protein
8g Fat	5g Fat
2g Sugar	2g Sugar

Sauté Medallions

Serves 2

Ingredients
4 Beef Medallions
1tsp vegetable oil
1 packet Brown Gravy mix
Instant Mashed Potatoes
Green Vegetable (Canned or Fresh)

Trim meat into four, 2in by 2in, medallions. Season with a pinch of salt and pepper sprinkled over the top of the medallions.

Begin the mashed potatoes by following the instructions on the box for two servings. After putting the water to boil for the potatoes heat 1 tsp vegetable oil in a skillet. Carefully place cutlets in the skillet.

Prepare the brown gravy by following the instructions on the package.

Allow meat to cook half way through on one side then turn the meat to cook the other side.

Prepare desired vegetables.
Plate and spoon gravy over meat and potatoes then serve.

Nutritional information
530 Calories
24g Protein
25 g Carbs
13g Fat
3g Sugar

Red Enchiladas

Serves 2

Ingredients
4 Thick Corn Tortillas
½ lb. Extra Lean Ground Beed
1 Cup Bueno Red Chili Puree
1 Cup Long Grain White Rice
1 Can Pinto Beans
1 Colby Cheese (1/2in. slice)
1 Can (4ozs) Tomato Sauce
½ Medium Onion
½ Tomato Sliced
2 Leaves of Romaine Lettuce
2 tbsps. Vegetable Oil
1 tbsp. Flour
2 Cups Water

Let thaw the red chili puree. Peel and cut the ½ onion in two. Cut

¼ of onion into strips and the other ¼ finely diced. Dice the

tomato. Grate the cheese. Cut the Romaine lettuce leaves into ¼

inch squares. Place the vegetables (except the strips of onions) next

to each other on a plate without mixing them. Wrap the corn

tortillas in plastic wrap and have them ready to place in microwave

once everything else is prepared.

In a medium saucepan heat, the vegetable oil. Toss in the onion

strips and rice. Stir until well covered with the oil and lightly

browned. Ass the water and tomato sauce. Mix well, stir

occasionally and allow to come to a fast boil. Reduce heat to less

than simmer and cover with lid. Let it cook for about 10 minutes

and then turn off heat and let the rice sit to one side on the stove.

Do not uncover at this point.

While the rice is cooking, put the ground beef in a skillet and stir

around to cook evenly. Once the meat is cooked, remove from

heat, drain excess fat and set aside.

In another sauce pan, heat the oil, add the flour and mix together

into a paste. Stir in the red chili puree quickly working the paste

into the chili to keep it from clumping. Stir constantly, add a little

salt to taste and bring to a simmer until the chili is hot.

Note: The flour paste is for thickening the chili sauce and cam be

omitted if desired. Also, a dash of garlic powder and a pinch of

oregano can be added for additional flavor.

Heat the Pinto beans and place the corn tortillas in the microwave for about 1 minute or until thoroughly warmed. On two dinner plates, place the tortillas and spoon a little ground meat at the center and roll, 2 on each plate. Pour the chili sauce across the top of the enchiladas. Sprinkle the dices onions and grated cheese on top of the enchiladas. Add next to the enchiladas a spoon full of rice, beans, lettuce, and tomato on top. "VOILA!!" A decent plate of heart friendly enchiladas! Enjoy!

Nutritional information
700 Calories per serving
38g Protein
42g Carbs
23g Fats
6g Sugar

A-1 Lime Steak and Bake
Serves 2

Ingredients
10oz. Steak
2 Medium size Russet Potatoes
1 Carrot
1 Tomato
1 Lime
Romaine Lettuce
¼ Cup (4oz) Worcestershire Sauce
1 tbsp. A-1 Steak Sauce
1 tsp. onion powder
1 tsp. garlic powder

In a small mixing bowl mix together ½ cup Worcestershire Sauce, 1 tbsp. A-1 sauce, and cutting the lime into quarter slices squeeze juice into mixture. Add 1 tsp. onion powder and 1 tsp. garlic powder, mix well. Place the steak in the bowl and make sure it is covered completely with the marinate mixture. Cover and refrigerate for 30 minutes or overnight according to desired seasoning strength.

Core and cut tomato into eighths. Shave carrots, cut off ends, and slice. Break about 6 leaves of the Romaine lettuce and cut into 1 inch squares. Toss vegetables together in a small bowl and place in the refrigerator until serving time.

Preheat oven to 350 degrees.

Wash the potatoes well. With a fork poke holes (2 or 3 times) on eh potatoes and wrap in foil. Bake the potatoes for about 15 minutes or until soft when squeezed a little at the center.

Once the potatoes are in the oven, start the grill and place the steaks on it. Cook to desired doneness, split in half, and serve.

Nutritional information
459 Calories
35g Protein
27g Carbs
20g Fat
3g Sugar

Just Chicken

<u>Rosemary Chicken with Roasted New Potatoes</u>
<u>Serves 2</u>

<u>Ingredients</u>
2 Thin Cut Skinless Chicken Breasts
4 New Potatoes
Thyme
Rosemary
Desired Green Vegetable(s)
Preheat oven to 375 degrees. Wash potatoes, cut with skin-on into
¾ inch squares. Soak in cold water to prevent discoloration.
Seasoning mix for the potatoes:
1 tsp garlic powder
½ tsp salt
½ tsp pepper
½ tsp parsley flakes
On a piece of foil spread the seasoning mix. Dry the potatoes and
roll in seasoning mix. Place on the cookie sheet. Bake in the oven
until fork tender.

Once the potatoes are in the oven, season the chicken with thyme,
rosemary, salt, and pepper. Place on the grill. Cook chicken
thoroughly until all the red/pink is gone and the meat is tenderly
white.
Heat the green vegetables.

Nutritional information
400 Calories per serving
24g Protein
32g Carbs
13g Fat
6g Sugar

Lemon Pepper Chicken/ Roasted Red Potatoes

Serves 2

Ingredients
2 Chicken Fillets
4 Red Potatoes
Desired Green Vegetables (canned or fresh)

Preheat oven to 375 degrees. Wash potatoes, cut with skin-on into ¾ inch squares. Soak in cold water to prevent discoloration. Fire up the grill and allow to heat while making the mix for the potatoes.

Seasoning mix for the potatoes:
1 tsp garlic powder
½ tsp salt
½ tsp pepper
½ tsp parsley flakes

Season the chicken breast by sprinkling lemon pepper across the tops.

On a piece of foil spread the seasoning mix. Dry the potatoes and roll in seasoning mix. Place on the cookie sheet. Bake in the oven until fork tender.

Once the potatoes are in the oven, put the chicken on the grill. Cook chicken thoroughly until all the red/pink is gone and the meat is tenderly white.

Heat the green vegetables about 5 minutes before removing the chicken from the grill.

Plate and serve.

Nutritional information
360 Calories
41g Protein
31g Carbs
7g Fat
6g Sugar

Grilled Chicken Penne
Serves 2

<u>Ingredients</u>
2 Chicken Breast Fillets
Penne Pasta
Desired Spaghetti Sauce
Fat Free Italian Dressing

Marinate chicken breast in 1 cup (8oz) of Fat Free Italian Dressing for minimum one hour, overnight if possible.

Start the water to boil for the Penne Pasta

Fire up the grill or preheat the George Foreman.

When the water comes to a fast boil, put in two handfuls of the Penne Pasta.

When the grill is hot, put the chicken on it to cook.

Heat the spaghetti sauce, 1 ½ cups should be sufficient.

The pasta is done when it is tender and rips in half when you pinch it. Drain and divide the pasta on to two plates.

Pour about a spoon and a half of the sauce atop the pasta. Cut the chicken into strips and place on top of the sauce.

Nutritional information
515 Calories
47g Protein
54g Carbs
12.5g Fat
10g Sugar

Chicken Wrap
Serves 2

Ingredients
2 Low-Carb tortillas
1 Chicken Breast Fillet
Lettuce
Tomato
Fat Free Mayonnaise
Lemon Pepper

Rub lemon pepper across the top of the chicken and grill chicken thoroughly.

Core tomato use ¼ tomato, slice tomato into pizza shapes.

Wash the lettuce and shred 1 cup.

Lay out 2 tortillas and spread 1 tsp. Mayonnaise onto the tortillas.

In the center of the wrap place equal parts lettuce and tomatoes onto the Mayonnaise. Carefully cut chicken into halves and then into strips. Place one half of chicken into each wrap.

Fold the two end and ENJOY!

Nutritional information for 1 Serving
195 Calories
9g Carb
18g Protein
6.5g Fat
1g Sugar

Chicken Salad Sandwich
Serves 2

Ingredients
1 Can of Chicken or Tuna
Fat Free Mayonnaise
2 hardboiled Eggs
Tomato
Lettuce
Diced Celery (optional)
1 small can Diced Olives (optional)
4 slices of Whole Wheat Bread

In a 1-quart pan, gently place two eggs in the pot and fill with water. Bring eggs and water to a fast boil. Boil eggs for 8-10 minutes, then drain, and allow to cool. Once cool enough to handle safely, peel and slice the eggs.

Wash lettuce, celery, and tomato. Dice half a stick of celery and half of the tomato.

Shred 2 large leaves. Open and drain a small can of diced olives and the can of chicken/tuna.

In a small mixing bowl drop in celery, tomato, olives, chicken/tuna, and eggs. Add 3 tbsp. Fat-Free Mayonnaise (more or less to taste as needed). Mix everything together and spread on 2 slices of whole wheat bread. Top with lettuce and cover with the other piece of bread.

Cut sandwiches if desired and serve.

Nutritional information for 1 Sandwich

Chicken
260 Calories
13g Carbs
21g Protein
8.5g Fat
4g Sugars

Tuna
260 Calories
13g Carbs
25g Protein
7g Fat
4g Sugars

9. *REST AND HEAT*

We have several people who suffer from sleep apnea, depression, and a variety of other health conditions brought on by being overweight. We have proven to them the benefits of a cardiovascular exercise, the use of Infrared Saunas, weight lifting, and a proper nutritional plan did make them feel better and resulted in 5-15 pounds of body fat off their weight in 7 weeks.

The amount of rest and sleep is an important component of our life. The best time for recovery from stress, life, and exercise is during our sleep patterns. Sleep is a time to rejuvenate us physically, mentally, emotionally, and spiritually. If you can make it a goal to try and **get 6-8 hours of deep**, uninterrupted sleep you will see faster changes. A deeper sleep can help release growth hormones, which can help put your body into a fat burning mode. These are also considered an anti-aging hormone.

The effect of not getting enough sleep is just the opposite. When you do not get enough sleep it affects the hormone production in a negative way. If the hormones Cortisol, Ghrelin, and Melatonin are improperly balanced it can affect your cardiovascular function, appetite, emotional moods, and sleep patterns.

.

10. QUICLEANSE NOTE'S

Why is it so important to look at my CALORIC intake? Your daily energy consists of a required caloric intake. Your resting metabolic rate, thermo genesis, and physical activity are the major factors that determine your daily needs. If you are less active then you don't want to eat as though you are running a marathon otherwise you input will not match the output (energy release) your body will store the leftovers and we all know where that goes, visceral body fat.

Let's go over why it is important to calculate the calories. It takes 3,500 calories to burn off 1 pound of fat. So if you eat a daily amount of 1,500 calories then you would have to burn (exercise, walk, swim, or run) off more than that amount of calories to burn off excess weight. When the total amount exceeds 3,500 you would have taken 1 pound of fat off. The opposite is true for building muscle. When building muscle, you would have to eat more than your daily caloric intake to gain muscle mass. Here are some numbers to keep up with once you have your proper daily

caloric intake:

1 gram of sugar = 4 calories

1 gram of protein = 4 calories

1 gram of carbohydrate = 4 calories

1 gram of fat = 9

<u>NOTES:</u>

GUIDE TO CARBOHYDRATES
(GI = Glycemic Index

	HIGH GI Carbs. (Breakfast)	MODERATE GI Carbs. (Lunch)	LOW GI Carbs. (Dinner)
FRUIT	Raisins Bananas (ripe)	Grapes Watermelon Mangos Kiwi	Berries Apples Pears Barley
VEGETABLES	Potato French fries (baked) Sweet Corn	Carrots Corn on the Cob Lima beans Yams	Asparagus Black Beans Lettuce (all types)
GRAINS	White bread Whole wheat bread Bagels Breakfast cereals Burger/hotdog buns White rice Pancakes	Brown rice Oatmeal Most pastas Popcorn Sourdough Bread	All bran cereals Whole grain bread Whole grain pasta Wild rice
DAIRY	Ice cream	Custard	Organic milk Organic plain yogurt Low-fat cottage cheese
BEVERAGES	Soft drinks Sport drinks Carrot Juice	Apple juice Orange juice	Fresh vegetable juice Grapefruit juice Green tea Water (8 glasses per day)
SWEETENERS	Corn syrup solids Sucrose (table sugar) Maltodextrin Maltose High-fructose corn syrup	Unrefined raw honey Organic brown sugar Barley malt Organic maple syrup	Fructose Stevia Splenda

ABOUT THE AUTHOR'S

Joey Gallardo is the eldest of the two brothers. Both Joey and Andy began their athleticism at young ages playing soccer. Joey, a collegiate soccer player and fitness trainer; has over 20 years of experience training individuals and assisting in their nutrition. Joey has owned his gym for 9 years and continues to motivate and inspire health and wellness.

Andy Gallardo, also played soccer most of his early life . He has a background in massage therapy, personal training, soccer coaching at various levels, and continues to educate individuals on proper nutrition and healthy living.

Family has always been a priority for the brothers and they continue to maintain close bonds and contact with several generations of family. Andy continues to utilize his business skills and passions for healthy living within his ongoing businesses in Las Cruces, NM. Joey continues to run his gym in Austin, TX and inspire individuals every day to be healthy and live happy. The brothers grew up in the city of El Paso, TX. Their parents still live in the same home they were raised in.

,

Printed in Great Britain
by Amazon

55719420R00035